Life

REFLECTIONS & JOURNAL

Lisa Nalbone

Illustrated by
Carrie Svozil

Text © 2016 by Lisa Nalbone
Illustration © 2016 by Carrie Svozil
All rights reserved.

No part of this publication may be reproduced
or transmitted in any form or by any means,
without permission in writing from the author.

Published in the United States by Lisa Nalbone
www.lisanalbone.com

ISBN 978-1-944983-00-0

Cover, Illustrations and book design by Carrie Svozil

Dear Megan ~
Thank you for
your kind
heart,
xo,
li

lisanalbone@gmail.com

Ask for help. Ask for advice.
Be willing to reach out and ask.
Ask: family, friends, neighbors, strangers, people at the park,
famous people, unknown people,
your network, the internet, me!
Just ask!
Even if it seems a bit scary. Or vulnerable. Or presumptuous.
What do I mean, ask? Ask for what?
Ask for: information, help, ideas, suggestions, an introduction to
a possible mentor, book and field trip recommendations,
favorite resources, a music teacher or coach.
Ask how they learned something.
Ask how they solved a problem you are having.
Ask for their story.
You help others feel valued when you ask for their advice.
You might learn the answer to your questions.
Or you might discover something completely different you didn't
realize you needed or wanted to learn.

ASK!

Begin

Start. Pick something you've always wanted to learn and begin.
Something new you are curious about?
Something your child asked? Whatever the subject, begin.
Don't worry, breathe and take a bite-sized step.
It doesn't have to be a serious subject
or part of any curriculum.
Not sure? Don't have it all planned out?
Never done it before? Doesn't matter.
Just begin. Blaze a new trail.
Once you start, you'll gain a better idea of how to proceed.
You can start learning on your own.
You might decide you want to find a teacher, mentor, or guide.
Learning beyond school
doesn't mean learning alone, without help.
You are born to learn. Some things might require more
conscious and consistent effort, but learning is part of what
we humans do, young, old, and in-between.
So, pick a topic and exercise those learning muscles.

BEGIN!

Yes, you! Create.
Or your kids, let them create!
Create things that demonstrate what you are learning about.
Create meals, recipes, art, wild & crazy things, useful and
practical things: clothing, furniture, a solution, a system for
keeping up with tasks. Endless possibilities!
Create connections
Connect with people, locally or globally, with ideas, about ideas
and for learning, progressing, discussing, creating. Create
communities for learning and doing.
Fearful you might make a mistake? You might,
but you'll learn how to do better next time.
Create courage and confidence.
You build courage and confidence as you create, take risks,
and follow through on your ideas.
You also create new reasons to celebrate and connect.
So, what are you waiting for?

CREATE!

discuss

Discuss ideas.

Discuss decisions, reasons,

why and how you do things.

Discuss news, politics, books--whatever you are learning.

Discuss in person, on Skype, on a forum, on Twitter.

Discover new ideas, dig into a topic,

distill your thoughts, and then discuss.

Discuss dreams, yours and others.

Dream about what you want to do.

Don't sit on the sidelines

and let those ideas and dreams dwindle away.

Discuss your dreams and

then decide, go, and do.

DISCUSS!

Explore new options and possibilities.
Explore a variety of paths and potential solutions before
making a decision. Explore new places and new people.
Explore new activities you never thought you'd like
or even try: flash mob anyone?
Experiment as you explore to learn what you enjoy and do well.
Explore new museums, cuisines, music, libraries, bookstores.
What can you delve into that is unchartered territory for you?
Explore new topics and publications, online or in hand,
in different fields of science, genres of literature,
alternatives for politics, religion, and analysis.
Explore and experiment with different approaches
to thinking, learning, and life.
Explore on your own or with friends
or partners, locally or virtually.
Explore new ways to learn, connect, and
put yourself out in the world.
Explore and expand beyond your typical borders. Get out of
your town, state, country, or off your continent!

EXPLORE!

Facilitate: Help make things happen for yourself and for others.

Fail: Fail fearlessly, pick yourself up, learn from your mistakes, and try again.

Fantasize: Fantasize about all the possibilities for change, growth, and learning

Finish: Finish, feel the satisfaction of persistence, completion and mastery.

Flourish: Flourish at home and in the world--dare to grow beyond other's limits
Find your path and flow and feast on an abundance of resources.

Follow-through: Follow-through on your ideas, tasks, and commitments.

Forget and Forgive: Forget and face your fears. Forgive those who just don't
get it and are stuck in old paradigms. Forgive yourself.

Found: Found a business, an organization, a family, a future, a fund for dreams.

Forward: Move; progress not perfection is the goal.

Free: Free yourself and your child from expectations and limitations.

Frequent: Frequently frequent places that make your heart sing!

Friend: Friend new people with interesting ideas. Find old friends. Friend loyally

F!

Go to a gathering, park, potluck, gallery,
meeting, performance, or exhibit.
Pack up the barest essentials and go.
Go on vacation, a trip, a hike, or an adventure.
If you forget something, oh well.
Most things can be gotten one way or another
if absolutely necessary. So, just go.
Give yourself permission to go.
Don't give in to fears and excuses.
Give others permission to go.
Go gratefully.
Go giggling.
Go and give generously.

GO!

Be honest in all you do. Commit to honesty and integrity.
Be radically honest so you can build trust.
Be honest about who you are, your biases, and your expectations.
Be honest about your blind spots, your strengths, and your weaknesses
Be honest and dare to see clearly who your child really is.
Be honest about and celebrate
your child's strengths, talents, weaknesses, quirks.
Be honest about your choices; why you do things and why you don't.
No excuses!
Help yourself, your family, and the world by making honesty a habit.
Help others be honest and true to themselves.
Be heroic by spreading honesty and hope.
When we honestly see others, and ourselves,
then we can trust and bring our truest selves to the world.
We can build confidence and connection.
When we give our children and ourselves the gifts of candor,
acceptance, and unconditional love,
we have the power to help ourselves and others heal.

BE HONEST!

Invite

Invite someone out for coffee, or over for a meal.
Invite someone along for the ride,
wherever you have decided to GO.
Invite new ideas, discussion, feedback, and collaboration.
Invite others to a learning circle, book group,
mastermind group, support group, or playgroup.
Imagine all the possibilities.
Interview those you invite, informally or formally,
and learn from their experiences.
Invite others to share your learning and their ideas.
Introduce each other to new people,
innovations, or information.
Invite imagination, ingenuity, and inspiration into your life.

INVITE!

Journey within and beyond.
Judge thoughtfully which goals, influences, and
destinations are right for you.
Juggle your time judiciously.
You may have to jury-rig and jumble along the way.
Just because you have begun,
the path won't necessarily be obvious or easy,
Join with others on a similar learning journey.
Journey through sorrows,
over challenges,
and with joy.

JOURNEY!

Keep going.
Learning beyond school may not be easy,
but it's a lifelong, worthy quest.
Keep your nose to the grindstone.
Even when the going gets rough, you encounter resistance,
or your energy flags, keep your chin up.
Keep your distance from naysayers
who close gates and say, "You can't."
Keep your cool when you must interact.
Keep in touch.
Keep close to your true friends, supporters,
and other lovers of learning who get it,
who understand the drive to learn your way.
Keep each other accountable.
Keep a place of refuge and rest.
Keep a sanctuary for your soul.
Keep your eyes on the prize.

KEEP!

Listen to learn, connect, and love.
Learn to listen, really listen, without reacting.
Listening skills are something you can keep on
learning, modifying, and improving.
Listening, like so many skills, is best learned by doing.
Listen with empathy. Try to listen without preconceived
notions, or thinking about what YOU want to say.
Listen lovingly, openly, and non-judgmentally.
Listen to folks with different kinds of
experiences, backgrounds, and viewpoints.
Listening actively is a powerful, not passive, skill.
Listen to yourself, your inner voice.
Listen to nature, stillness, and quiet.
Consider what you have learned from your listening.
Then listen to your heart. Act on things which
are true and help you live, laugh, love, and learn.

LISTEN!

Make learning meaningful and fun.

Make mistakes and messes and music and meals.

Make memories.

Make mindfulness and

movement a part of every day.

Make decisions.

Make the effort.

Make things happen.

Make a difference.

MAKE!

Network to connect, share, give, and learn.
Network to give freely with no expectation of getting.
Focus on how you can serve and help others.
Network with other learners, parents, and mentors
to share ideas, tips, and encouragement.
Network with professionals, authors, scholars, and
potential mentors in fields of interest or study.
Network in person at conferences,
events, or in your neighborhood.
Network on the net with
Twitter, Facebook, LinkedIn, blogs.
Strive to make your network broad, deep, and diverse.
Enrich and strengthen your networks as a source of support,
learning, creativity, action, accountability and generosity.
Nurture networks. Help them form. Share them.

NETWORK!

Open your eyes and observe.

Open your heart to finding and following your path.

Open your mind to learning in new and myriad ways.

Open doors to new opportunities and change.

Open your arms and embrace the uncertainty.

Open your hands and offer your gifts to the world.

Open gateways, windows, latches, enclosures.

Open wide outside or self-imposed limitations.

Open yourself to original options to overcome obstacles.

Or, as Ali Baba says, "Open Sesame"

OPEN!

PLAY

Please, oh please, play every day.

Play inside and outside and every which way.

Plan a party, play music, or perform in some plays.

Playing is learning, it's not just a craze.

You might solve problems, paint pictures, or find new ways

To make peace, persevere, or get through a maze.

Playing can lead to your passion or path,

Help reduce stress and make you laugh.

I'm up on my pedestal and just have to say,

Parents and children you really must play.

PLAY!

Question to quench your thirst for knowledge
and quicken your curiosity.
Question authority, the status quo,
information providers, power, and money.
Question reasons, background, goals,
systems, and underlying beliefs.
Query loudly, if needed, and don't be afraid to ask:

"Who, what, where, when, how, and WHY, WHY, WHY?"

Question quality and quantity.
Question quietly, thoughtfully, reflectively.
Question yourself daily, "Am I doing what matters?"
Quietly take some time to listen.

QUESTION!

read

Read aloud
Read in bed, read
between the lines
Read 'cause you can
Read dreary doctrines.

Read every day!
Read the fine print, read for fun
and with friends.
Read Google and giggle,
Read hard covers
to get through hard times.

Read into.
Read journals
Read Kant, if you're inclined.
Read literature, for leisure and
laughing good times.

Read mysteries,
Read non-fiction.
Read often.
Read poetry, prose, and
piteously poor rhymes.

Read quotations
Read reflections and research
Read seriously
Read topics telling the times.

Read under covers.
Read voraciously to verify.
Read widely.
Read while drinking good wines.

Read in Xanadu .
Read year-round,
Read zealously.

Read for joy and discovery
and to be you
at all times.

READ!

Share

Share what you learn,
Share what you play.
Share what you read,
make, or explore any day.
Share your enthusiasm, wonder, and zest.
Share your doubts and fears
when you don't feel your best.
Share your gifts and your burdens,
as well as your wealth.
Life is so good
when you share yourself.

SHARE!

Trust yourself.
Trust your intuition, your inner voice, your gut.
Trust even when it's hard because
most people disagree with you.
Trust your children.
Trust in their ability to grow, to learn,
to know themselves and their feelings.
Trust that others have good intentions, but
you still may choose to trust your own decisions.
Trust the things that make your heart sing.
Trust that with intention, hard work, and
showing up you can always keep learning.
Trust that you will encounter confusion and difficulties.
Trust that if you are present, pay attention, and listen
you can figure out your next step.
Trust the learning process.

TRUST!

Unite with and bring together
friends and fellow self-directed learners.
Unite with your networks and neighbors.
Unite with ukulele enthusiasts.
(I had to include uke. I'm a uke convert!)
Unite with others ready to ask, try and do.
Unite to build community, get things done, and have fun.
Unite the usual with the unusual.
Random collisions can inspire and transform.
Unite to unwind, bring together, connect, and
unleash the power and joy of community.
Unite with one another for coffee or wine or
with an online community spanning the globe.
Unite to understand, to uplift, and
to keep going when unsure.

UNITE!

Volunteer and you'll learn in so many ways.
Volunteer once, or for years, or just a few days.
Volunteer when you're happy,
Volunteer when you're sad.
Volunteer even with little time to be had.
Volunteer for a cause that speaks to your heart.
Volunteer and you just might find a new start.
Volunteer on vacation, to visit, to help
with your time and your skills.
Volunteer–
you might find new friends
and work that fulfills.

VOLUNTEER!

Write *Write* Write *Write* **Write**

Write

Write *Write* **Write** Write **Write** Write

Write every day, write in some way.

Write while you work, Write while you play.

Write a love note, a blog, instructions, a book.

Write to think and reflect, to take a deeper look.

Write about what you're learning,

or wonder, or whom you meet.

Write thank-you notes, emails, and essays, and tweet.

Write to dream, to set goals, and to create.

Write on a schedule, or while you wait.

Write to share and record all you hold dear.

Write, and just let go of the fear.

Write, and you'll be amazed at the end of the year.

WRITE!

eXperience what you are learning, whenever you can.

eXperience to eXpand your thinking and your limits.

eXperience to reality check ideas and find new resources.

eXperience and eXplore new cities, countries, the world.

eXamine other's eXperiences and eXplanations.

eXperience new ways to learn and to

eXercise your body and mind.

eXPERIENCE!

When invitations, opportunities, new eXperiences
come your way, yell,
"Yes, I'll try that. Yes, I'm in!"

When challenges, obstacles, bumps,
or frustrations come along yell,
"Yes, I can deal with this. I can figure things out. Yes, I can."

When asked to commit to your beliefs and
go after your goals and dreams, yell,
"Yes, I will do what it takes. I will show up. Yes, I will."

Are you up for lifelong learning beyond school?

YELL YES!

Zzzz when you must, Zzzz when you can,
Zzzz on a schedule or nap with no plan.
Zzzz to keep up your zest and keep up your zeal.
Zzzz to help you remember and help you heal.
Zzzz to enjoy what you love and explore.
Zzzz to help cope as well as to soar.
Zzzz in a hammock, a park, or a bed.
Zzzz after lunch or before you've been fed.
Zzzzing is a great way to charge up your brain,
And help you to learn, again and again.
Zzzz on your own or with ones you love,
Zzzzing will help with all the above.
The secret of life is not too profound,
You must Zzzz enough, is what I have found.

ZZZZZZZZZ!

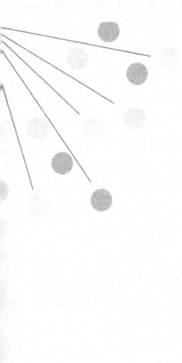

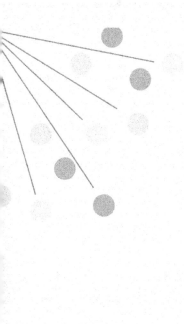

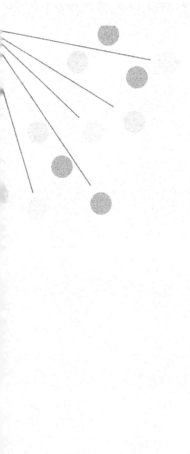

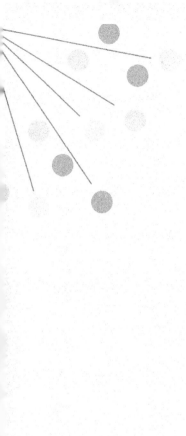

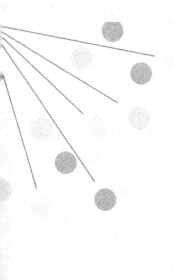

This journal was created during the collaboration between author Lisa Nalbone and artist Carrie Svozil, while they worked on the book and workbook both titled:

LifeSPARKS

ASK hard questions, TRY new things, DO what matters.

These books share insights and strategies to inspire and support a lifelong journey of joyful learning and courageous action. See www.lisanalbone.com for more resources and notification of other books publishing status.

Thanks for allowing us to join you on this journey.

Here's to lots of sparks!

CPSIA information can be obtained
at www.ICGtesting.com
Printed in the USA
FSOW04n0458080916
24693FS